How to

Master 13 Negotiating Skills

&

Win in Business

By

Shabbir Hossain

Copyright (C) 2016 CSB Academy Publishing Co.

All rights reserved. In accordance with the U.S. Copyright Act of 1976, the scanning, uploading, and electronic sharing of any part of this book without the permission of the publisher is unlawful piracy and theft of the author's intellectual property. If you would like to use material from this book (other than for review purposes), prior written permission must be obtained by contacting the publisher. Thank you for your support of the author's rights.

CSB Academy Publishing Company.

P. O. Box 966

Semmes, Alabama 36575, USA

Cover Design

By

David Miller

First Edition

Table of Contents

About me 3

Preface 5

Chapter 1: People Skills 11

    4 Behaviors Defined by DiSC 13

        1. Dominant Personality 13

        2. Influencer 13

        3. Steadiness 14

        4. Conscientious Personality 15

Chapter 2: Listening Skill 19

    3 Steps to Asking and Listening 20

        1. Know the Direction 20

        2. Ask the Questions 21

    3 Styles of Listening 22

        1. Selective Listening 22

        2. Responsive Listening 22

        3. Playback Style Listening 22

Chapter 3: Develop a Full Plan Before You Go to Negotiate ... 25

    6 Steps: A Great Plan 25

        1. Use DiSC and other Research Data 25

        2. Indentify Your Own Goal and Interests 26

3. Indentify Their Goal and Interests 26

4. Valuation of the Deal 27

5. Know How Much to Compromise 27

6. Know How Low You Will Go 28

Chapter 4: Know What You Want 30

Chapter 5: Knowing What They Want 36

    4 Steps to knowing what THEY Want 37

        1. Identify Their Interests 38

        2. Indentify their Walk-Away Limit 38

        3. Indentify the Decision Maker 41

        4. Indentify Their Strength and Weakness 41

Chapter 6: Knowing When to Walk Away 45

    3 Steps to Establishing Your BATNA 48

        1. Know your Price Range 48

        2. Know Their Price Range 48

        3. Know the Deal Breaker List 48

Chapter 7: Know How Much to Compromise 51

Chapter 8: Knowing the Barrier 53

Chapter 9: Knowing How to Control Your Emotion 59

Chapter 10: Using the Time (Clock) to Your Advantage 62

Chapter 11: Finding Mutual Gain 66

5 Basic Principles of Mutual Gain Negotiations 66

    1. Indentifying Mutual Interest 66

    2. Willingness to Work Together 66

    3. Agreeing on Standards 67

    4. All Options on the Table 67

    5. Build a Relationship 67

4 Steps to a Win-Win For Both Parties 68

    1. Good Preparation 68

    2. Create Value 68

    3. Coming to an Agreement 69

    4. Forecast Future Challenges 69

Chapter 12: Make Them Look Good, Let Them Brag 70

6 Ways to Make Them Look Good 70

    1. Win-Win Situation 70

    2. Allow Participation 71

    3. Acknowledge Their Interest 71

    4. Offer Options 71

    5. Offer to Help 72

    6. Make them Look Good 72

Chapter 13: The Power of Paper 73

3 Ways You Can Put Paper Power to Work for You 73

1. Following up 73

2. Show a Summery Deal 74

3. Sign the Purchase Agreement 74

Chapter 14: A Deal I Recently Negotiated 76

Here is a List of My Findings: 76

About the Businesses 76

About the Seller 77

11 Step Preparation Before the Meeting 79

SWOT Analysis Findings 81

About me

My name is Shabbir Hossain. I have been at gas stations and a few other retail businesses for the last 20 some years. I have a B.S. degree in Marketing from the University of South Alabama. In this 20 plus years, along with gas stations, I have also owned, managed, and/or operated a few other types of retail businesses like fast food franchises, an Italian restaurant, a pizza delivery business, a dry cleaner, B2B wholesaling, and even liquor stores. Every business I bought, sold or leased over the years has had some degree of negotiation involved. I have done everything from simple "handshake deals" to hardcore back and forth negotiation of commercial leases, from financing terms to pricing.

I fell into the consulting business two years ago without even knowing that I did it, when I was first approached by a group of investors for my help in negotiating a deal for 3 gas stations that they were trying to buy as part of their investment portfolio. It was a long process, but after 3 months I was able to make a deal happen where my investors ended up with a better deal than what they expected.

So my journey began as a business consultant, but this is not about my journey, but yours. And since the stakes are too high to lose when you are trying to get your first business deal, I want you to be a winner from the very first deal and on.

Over the years I have learned a few valuable lessons when it comes to business deal negotiation. Not all deals are the same, and the same negotiation skills do not always work in every deal. Each business deal is unique and comes with its own set of challenges.

Business Negotiation is one skill no one is born with, nor should you "learn on the go" because the stakes are too high. Looking back from my very first deal to the last one, the journey has been painfully long and, at times, it cost me dearly. But one thing I will say that most of the costly mistakes I made were limited to my early business life. It is certain that the more you do, the better you get at it.

In this book, I have summarized the 13 most vital "must have" skills that I've learned and practiced over the years on many deals. These are the very skills that most top negotiators use in big businesses. As you read them, you will see and understand why they are so vital and essential to every business negotiation.

In the event, if you need to contact me, feel free to send me an email at Shabbir@GasStationBusiness101.com

Good luck!

Preface

"I have not failed. I've just found 10,000 ways that won't work." - Thomas A. Edison

"Failure should be our teacher, not our undertaker. Failure is delay, not defeat. It is a temporary detour, not a dead-end. Failure is something we can avoid only by saying nothing, doing nothing, and being nothing." - Denis Waitley

There have been a few major failures in my 25 years of business that I have talked about on my podcast show a few times. Admitting my own failure isn't easy to do, but I knew in order to move on, I would have to face my failure, deal with it and put it behind me. But more importantly, analyze and pinpoint what and why I lost in those deals.

There is a valuable lesson to be learned in every failure. Although there is a very high cost, they are valuable, and I took them to heart. In 25 years I have owned, leased, operated, bought and sold over 20 different types of businesses. They have ranged from restaurant to wholesale route sales and everything in between. Looking back I can say with confidence that all the ones at which I was successful had one thing in common: a great negotiation that leads to a great deal either in the lease/rent or price. This is the most essential skill needed for any new business.

Looking back on the ones where I failed, I know where I went wrong. Again, they all had one thing in common: I was too eager and desperate to pay attention to the details and agreed too easily to the terms I was offered.

In order to get started on the right foot, you need a good negotiation with a good hard bargain. If you have this good start in your business, then you can use the momentum to carry you through the hard times we all face when starting any new business.

When I started in the business, there wasn't a mentor or a book to read that taught me how to actually negotiate in business. Rather, I did what came naturally to me. Little did I know that a common sense approach to business negotiations is not the best idea. It really is like a game of tough folks, where the one who doesn't blink wins. If this sounds strange, that's because it is strange but that's the reality. Over the years I learned to play the 'game of negotiation' well as I had to practice it often in various business ventures.

Not everyone is born with the skill of great business negotiation. Rather, it is a set of skills that you acquire through experience, by watching someone else do it through mentoring or reading a good book or two on 'How to negotiate in business,' and then you can practice and become a master at it.

The first and most important lesson in negotiation is never to show desperation, no matter what you are buying or selling, the smell of desperation can spread really fast and ruin any chance at winning a deal.

As I said before, we acquire this set of skills through learning, practicing and mastering each individual skillfully. While there are probably countless books, mentors, and masters out there on this subject, I was only able to read four books on this very topic myself. Those books were helpful to a degree, but since this is a very dynamic business world, I realized that the books alone wouldn't teach me what I needed. I needed to take the education from the books and combine that with my own real life experience and then come up with a set of skills of my very own. So in the end, I have developed a set of skills in business that were learned from the mistakes I made over the years and also from the deals I won.

I was also fortunate enough to follow and learn from a mentor (a great friend who works as a consultant for many big name investors, his niche is merger & acquisition) for almost a year. He is the person who helped me perfect my skill sets. Throughout my many years in business, I have always practiced what I preach.

As a business consultant in the gas station industry, investors often hire me to negotiate deals from start to finish.

My job is to prepare a set of business, marketing, and operation plans and help them to implement each plan at the right time in order to see them succeed.

This book isn't about MY success, but rather YOUR success. Keep in mind that the best lessons you will learn will come from your own life experience and often your own failed negotiation in business. I have had my fair share of failed negotiations, and I've learned a lot from each of them, but after watching my mentor negotiate deals, I noticed a pattern and started taking notes.

By the fifth deal, I knew my mentor's moves, but I also realized that he didn't approach every deal with the same tactics and skills and never in the same order. Rather each deal was different, and by this, I mean the order in which he used the 13 skills that will be discussed in this book. Every deal doesn't come with a cookie cutter pattern; each deal will vary, and at times my mentor showed me how not to implement all 13 skills since it would overkill a deal.

There is some basic legwork that you need to do before each deal or negotiation, even long before you go to the table and sit down. You need to collect some data by research and discovery ahead of time, so you can take the time to analyze it and then determine what your exact game plan is going to be.

I know this may sound confusing, but after I discuss all 13 skills sets, I will walk you through a real-life example of a negotiation that I had done recently and how these skills sets worked in that negotiation process. I will share the details and the outcome of the negotiation so you can visualize how these 13 skills work in real life business situations.

I have always been the type of student that learns best by examples because I'm a visual person; I need to visualize and relate to a real life situation in order to completely understand the problem. If you're like me, then you will enjoy reading the real life business negotiation story I share in the last chapter and can actually visualize how the process works.

Before we get into the 13 essential skills, just keep in mind what I've said. I've told you a lot, but there are two important things to note down or remember. Can you tell me what those two things are?

I told you:

1. The first lesson in negotiation, don't ever show desperation.

2. Research, discovery and data collection.

Why do research and what do we collect data on? We need to research the buyer/seller or whoever we are going to be negotiating with. We need all the data we can find about them: How much money do they have? How serious are they? How badly do they need this deal? What makes them like this deal? What may they not like about the deal? What can make this deal unique for them? What type of personality do they have? Are they hot or hard headed? Are they polite? What is their education level?

No, you don't need a 10-page research paper on them or on their personality; but you do need to understand who they are, how they work and what and how to influence them to buy/sell on this deal.

When you read about the next 13 skill sets, you will see how each and every bit of this research data will become useful. It is best to gather as much data as possible, and you can do this without being too obvious.

Don't start calling their friends and asking about how much money they have. This will just make you lose the deal for sure. Rather, be tactful and creative when it comes to your discovery and data collection. If you are dealing with someone smart, trust me... they are already doing the same on you.

Chapter 1: People Skills

One of the first things I learned while doing business negotiations is that you deal with a lot of different people. However, until I started doing this, I didn't quite realize how much my behavior can affect the behavior of others and the importance this plays on people skills in business negotiations.

Our external behavioral cues are determined by our attitude to a situation. When I go into a negotiation, I need to be aware that my attitude comes across in my smile, voice tone and use of words. If I were to send the wrong physical signals to the other party, then it could have a negative effect on their attitude, which could destroy the whole negotiation before it even gets started. This is why it is important to get to know the individual you are negotiating with before you even walk in the door. If I know the type of person I'm dealing with I can be better prepared for using the proper cues. To do this, I developed an understanding of the four DiSC or Dimensions of Behavior attributes and how they interact with each other.

First, let me explain this model. DiSC isn't a tool to help with your negotiating skills; rather it helps you to know how a person's behavior is affected when interacting with a specific environment like negotiating. This model helped me to identify my negotiating style and how others may view me. I also learned why I'm more comfortable negotiating with some people than others. If you are negotiating with someone who has a similar style, then the process will be much simpler. On the other hand, if I find myself negotiating with someone of a less compatible style then I know I'm going to have to spend more time persuading that person. So let's get on with looking at the four different behaviors defined by the DiSC model.

4 BEHAVIORS DEFINED BY DISC

1. Dominant Personality

The first behavior that you are likely to find in business is the dominant personality. These are the individuals who are good at making decisions and want to control the negotiating environment. When I deal with these types of individuals, I find they are very direct and good at telling it to you like it is. For those new to the negotiating business, facing a dominant personality can be very intimidating. Often when you deal with these people, they won't do well with questioning and listening skills. I find it is best to use a bottom line approach with the dominant personality since they tend to be goal driven and don't like to consider multiple solutions or outcomes. However, if something isn't going to work, you can be sure people with this personality trait will definitely tell you and this may make them seem negative at first. I always remember that when dealing with a dominant personality... focus more on problem-solving and meeting challenges and less on emotional feelings.

2. Influencer

Next, is the personality of the influencer. Like a dominant personality, these individuals will still tell you like it is; but with a less direct approach. In negotiations, these individuals are always trying to convince and motivate me to take a deal, rather than try to coerce me into the deal. While a dominant personality will focus on the tasks to get results, an influencer will focus more on the people. When I offer a deal to an influencer, I know they are going to focus more on the possibilities rather than the downfalls. The best approach I've found to working with these individuals is to strive for a favorable impression and focus on building a relationship with them. While these individuals may first come across as impulsive and disorganized, I realized they are just looking at the big picture rather than all the little details. I always remember when dealing with influencers to take a team approach to the deal.

3. Steadiness

Then there is the personality of steadiness. Again, I find these people look to the positive aspects of a deal when negotiating. However, I find these individuals the most difficult to work with since they tend not to like change even if it is for the best. The view of these individuals is that everything will work out if people just work hard together towards a common goal. I find these individuals are really good at listening and carefully consider things before giving me a reply. If you have a dominant or influence personality style, you will need to be careful since you will want an immediate response, but won't get one with this personality style. I find it best to be methodical and reserved when dealing with steadiness personalities.

4. Conscientious Personality

Lastly, there is the conscientious personality. As with a steadiness personality, these individuals tend to be introverted and reserved, although I find these individuals to be more task oriented and control focused like a dominant personality. If I'm dealing with a conscientious personality, I need to have a clearly defined point and back it up with factual statements. Many view these individuals as perfectionists with a very diplomatic and business-like approach. I won't win a deal with these individuals unless I support my reasons with a lot of facts.

So as you can see, it is important to know both your personality style and that of the individual you are going to be negotiating with. For example, if you are an influencer personality, and you are negotiating with a conscientious personality then you will need to have lots of accurate facts and supportive information. Alternately, if you have a dominant personality; it is important to remember to have patience when dealing with any other personality. Or if you are a conscientious personality then you need to be careful you don't come across as indecisive during negotiations.

As a negotiator, I find it important to have a complete picture of how an individual will behave and know the best way to communicate with them. I have found that when evaluating a person's personality style I need to consider the following nine items:

1. Goals
2. Emotions
3. Judgments
4. Influence
5. Value to the business
6. Overused tendencies
7. How they behave under pressure

8. Fears

9. How they increase their effectiveness

While I tend to use certain attributes more than others, because I'm more comfortable with some, I have realized that it is important to learn how to use all attributes in case they are needed. This is a very effective and important part of developing your negotiation skills.

If people with different personality styles interact, the experience can be either positive or negative. While a positive experience is good for everyone, I find it important to be prepared for any negative outcome, so I'm ready to turn it into a positive experience. This will help the other party in the negotiation to have a good experience as well and lead to a better chance of the deal getting approved.

For example, if you are an influencer, and you are dealing with a conscientious person you don't want to make a remark about the quality of a product and only have minor statistics to support your remark. The conscientious individual will question your remark, and you won't be able to support their level of standards. If you are a dominant, dealing with a conscientious person, you don't want to start talking to fill the silence while these individuals take the time to think. Pushing them for an answer or a decision will only lead to a negative experience for everyone and an unfinished deal. If you are an influencer dealing with a dominant, remember to use a short and direct approach rather than going into a story or anecdote. I know you may be thinking these examples are just minor details, but the fact is you can change and adapt these situations into a positive outcome and a closed deal if you are skilled at negotiating.

In order to improve your negotiating skills, the first thing I recommend is that you practice your people skills. To do this, I take the time not only to recognize the personality style of the individual or individuals I'm negotiating with but to also completely understand how my own tendencies influence the scene and what I can do to be more flexible at the negotiating table so that everyone walks away a winner.

Chapter 2: Listening Skill

In the previous chapter, I touched on the fact that a part of negotiating is learning about the person and their personality. In this chapter, I'm going to discuss one of the most important ways that you can learn this information. That's the powerful skill of listening. As you probably already determined, some of the personality styles I discussed earlier are better at this than others. Overall, the majority of individuals aren't good listeners. I know this was a skill I had to struggle with learning. I found my biggest problem area was that I thought I only needed to listen in order to make a reply, and then I learned that you need to listen to understand.

What helped me to truly understand this fact was an illustration of the ways individuals communicate. If there are two or more personality types involved in a negotiation, there are three primary ways people communicate. The biggest way is through body language, with the tone of voice coming in a close second and words only a small percentage. This helped me to realize why being a good listener is more than just hearing the words, but hearing what's not being directly said.

This doesn't mean you should just stop listening to the words and focus on other things. Rather you still need to focus on the questions you ask and pay attention to the actual words being said. However, if there is a difference in the words someone is saying, then the body language and tone of voice play an important role in how we communicate. I always keep in mind the statistic that 93% of communication is non-verbal. That makes it a big part of your negotiation, and it also helps to realize why a lot is lost between what is said and what is heard. It is also important to determine the speaker's style in order to get a better handle on their non-verbal communication.

The primary way that you can learn the interests of the other negotiating party is to use questions. I find that learning to ask the right questions at the right time is an important part of developing effective negotiating skills. In order to ask the right questions, I find there are three things that you need to do.

3 STEPS TO ASKING AND LISTENING
1. Know the Direction

First, understand where you want your questions to go. Don't just ask random questions. Rather you want to ask a question with a purpose and know where you are going to go next after you get your answer. If you don't know this in advance, you are going to unnerve the other individual, and this will just create a level of distrust between you.

2. Ask the Questions

Second, before you start, always take the time to ask the other party if they don't mind you asking questions. Most of the time, both parties are going to be asking a lot of questions. However, you never know if you are dealing with someone who may prefer another party to answer your questions. Don't waste time asking questions of the wrong person.

3. Stay on Topic

Lastly, make it clear what information you want to know. This shows the other party that you have a reason behind your questions. Then make sure you keep your questions on topic and take them in the direction you want to go. This will put the other party at ease and help them to trust you.

Now that you are prepared to get the necessary information, I need to tell you how to listen appropriately. When it comes to listening, I found there are three styles. You want to use a combination of all three styles and use them appropriately to gain relevant information about the other negotiating party.

3 STYLES OF LISTENING

1. Selective Listening

The first listening style is selective. This is a relatively simple style to explain; basically, this is where you hear what you want to hear. This means you are hearing what you think is relevant and ignoring any other things you hear whether they be verbal or non-verbal.

2. Responsive Listening

The second style is responsive. This style is important because it allows the other negotiating party to know that you are actually paying attention to what is being said. You want to focus on both your verbal and physical feedback when implementing this style. You can ask for clarification or simply nod to show the other person you are focused on what they are saying.

3. Playback Style Listening

Lastly, there is the playback style. This is my favorite listening style since you restate what you think you heard and get confirmation. You can also follow up with a confirmation question if needed. The reason this is my favorite is because it tends to combine the previous two listening styles. You show the other individual that you are actually listening and focused on them while also allowing you to get confirmation that you got the information correct.

As you work through a negotiation process, it is a good idea to use this playback listening style during the close. Not only can this help you to make sure everything was understood properly, but it will also make it more difficult for issues to resurface later. This way you can clarify and work through issues before closing and having to come back to it later; making it seem as if you weren't listening during the initial negotiating process.

After I've talked to you about listening and questioning, it is easy to see how these skills can help you solve a variety of negotiation problems. When you encourage the other party to talk, and you listen carefully to their replies, you are sending a positive message to them, and as I discussed in the first chapter, a positive message is important no matter what personality style you are dealing with. When you send a positive message to the other party, you are enhancing their trust in you, and you are reducing the common tensions that arise during a negotiation.

I find that when you use good listening skills as a part of negotiating you will be able to do business with a larger variety of people since they will perceive you as being trustworthy, adequate at problem-solving and see you as bringing value to the negotiation process. These perceptions are increased as you develop a strong listening skill.

Chapter 3: Develop a Full Plan Before You Go to Negotiate

Now that I've discussed the two important parts of preparing to negotiate, it is time to discuss what you do with the information you gained. After you've learned about the other person's personality style and listened carefully to determine what their focus and goals are, you want to put all of this information together and develop an in-depth plan before you go in for the negotiation. I don't simply mean planning on how much is spent, how long the project will take or what a walk-away number might be; rather I'm talking about a detailed plan that will attempt to touch on everything that the other side may want and why. For an effective, detailed plan I find there are six specific steps you want to follow.

6 STEPS: A GREAT PLAN

1. Use DiSC and other Research Data

As I discussed in the first chapter, the first step in developing a full plan is to determine the negotiating style of the other party. Using the DiSC style and some research you can easily find out the personality style of the individual or individuals you are negotiating with and this will help you determine how you are going to communicate with them. If you can't find the style of the other individual you can always make an educated guess and then adjust as the negotiation proceeds. However, I highly recommend you take the time to learn the person's style before deciding to just go in and wing it, since it offers a better chance of success.

2. Indentify Your Own Goal and Interests

The second step in your planning should be identifying what your own interests are. I'm not saying you simply need to determine what you want. It goes beyond that. You want to determine why you want what you want. You will likely find that you have more than one interest as I did, and that is okay, just make sure you scrutinize them all.

3. Indentify Their Goal and Interests

Third, determine the interests of the other party or business. This is a major part of your negotiating process. If I don't know what the other party wants and why, then I can't be effective at negotiating and leading them in the direction I want to go. Knowing the other party's interests help you to find goals you have in common and goals that are in opposition. I find this helpful because I can spend less time focusing on negotiating something we already have in common and more time trying to iron out something we are in opposition on so that we can win the negotiation.

4. Valuation of the Deal

Determining value is the fourth step in developing your plan. This includes the value of what you have to offer and what the other side is likely to view as valuable. I need to make sure I'm offering something of lesser value to me, but high value to the other side while also getting something valuable from the other side that they view as of a lesser value to them. This is the give and take part of the negotiating process, and it is a very stressful period. I found having a good plan in advance can certainly make this time a lot less stressful.

Another thing I've found is that those without strong negotiating skills tend to overlook this part of the planning process. If you don't take the time to consider and set this up then you need to be prepared to make a lot of last-minute compromises and these can sometimes turn out bad for you and your company.

5. Know How Much to Compromise

Fifth, you want to brainstorm some ideas for how to implement a good negotiation process. I've learned that negotiating is more about joint problem solving than simply making compromises. The key is you need to know how to move the negotiation from a series of compromises to a joint problem-solving. The easiest way to do this is use phrases that involve the term "we." So look at the above steps in the planning and learn to make phrases like "What if we did this?" or "What if we tried...?" before making any offers and you will be surprised how well negotiating goes for you. I know I was.

6. Know How Low You Will Go

The last step in the plan is probably your easiest and is the only step in the process that you may be able to answer with a simple question. You want to have a least acceptable line that you won't cross. If you work for a company, this may already be established for you, or you may need to come up with this on your own. Whatever you do, just don't be afraid to walk away from the deal if you get to this line. Setting boundaries are very important in negotiating, and you may not want to walk away, but believe me... the other side is ready to.

Let's look at that last step a little closer. When I first heard BATNA or Best Alternative to a Negotiated Agreement, I wasn't entirely sure what was involved. Then I learned that this is one of the most vital components to developing a strong set of negotiating skills. The mindset to have is that you don't want to accept an outcome that is worse than what may have happened if you hadn't accepted the agreement.

Basically, establishing a BATNA is stating what you will do if you cannot reach an agreement during the negotiation process. What you plan in the sixth stage of the process needs to be of greater value that what you establish for your BATNA, otherwise there would be no point in negotiating. You should also consider what the BATNA of the other side is since this will help you determine why they are negotiating with you and what is preventing them from finding another source. This will be valuable in staying within everyone's bounds and finding a solution for both negotiating parties.

Let me leave you with another statistic I learned that really opened my eyes. A reader poll in Negotiator Magazine for 2004 found that nearly 40% of the negotiating process is done internally. This is why planning is so important since it works out the internal part of the negotiating process before you enter formal negotiations, so you don't end up figuring it out as you go along. I find this is helpful in avoiding an unacceptable outcome and gives me a chance to focus on the most important parts of the formal negotiating process to get the best possible deal.

Chapter 4: Know What You Want

"Knowing what you want is also knowing how much you are willing to give up to get it."

Now that we have discussed researching and planning, there is another thing you need to be ready for. You need to think of yourself and know exactly what it is you want out of the negotiation. I was surprised at how easily you can get caught up in preparing for everything the other side might do and actually forget to focus on what you want and what direction you will go. Consider the following tips I've learned to help you negotiate a great deal and get what you want.

Perhaps the first thing you want to do is establish what you are willing to concede. I know this may seem like a contradiction. Why do you want to know what you will get rid of when you are supposed to be negotiating to get something? This is because you need to know your bottom line and know your minimums before you start the negotiation process. Negotiating can be an exciting time, and you may be tempted to make a concession that you weren't prepared for in order to close the deal, only to find later you went too low for your deal. So make sure you establish a clear bottom line early on in the planning process.

Along this line, I want to also put out the warning that you should never assume anything. You are likely going to head into a negotiation with certain expectations about what is possible, and this may hold you back from certain tactics. However, as I will discuss later, it is important to consider how emotions affect your behavior since you want to have a broad perspective on what can be negotiated. While you have done a lot of research and planning before going into the negotiation, you don't want to presume you already know all of the issues, what the other party wants, and how the negotiation process is going to go. Detailed planning and preparation go a long way to knowing everything, but it doesn't mean you have planned for every possible outcome, it just means you are ready to make the right split-second decision and know when to change.

Just as important, I find it is good to deal with the right people. I try not to deal with subordinates, but to only deal with those individuals who have the power and authority to close a deal as we negotiate. I don't want to spend all this time working out an agreement only to have it stop because we need to wait for someone in management to approve the deal. Ask to negotiate with someone at the top so you don't waste your time and can finalize without any delay.

I also want to add a warning here. When you are considering what you want from a negotiation, I don't just think in terms of money. Rather, I always try to remember to include a timeline and expectation in the planning process. I've seen many negotiations fall apart later because the actual timeline for implementation is just added as an afterthought. It is important to consider your time line as a part of the initial agreement so that everyone can have a realistic expectation of what is going to be accomplished. So when it comes to knowing what you want, make sure you have a detail of benchmarks, timeline, and a payment schedule if needed so you can manage all expectations.

I know the popular myth where people say you should create certain value for your offer, but that is not always the key factor in a negotiation. Don't get me wrong, creating value is certainly an important part of the negotiation process, but it shouldn't be your primary focus. What I mean by this is you don't want to focus so much on creating value in your offer that you forget your ability to claim your value.

I'm not trying to say you should go around bragging about yourself and your offer, or refusing to consider alternatives. I'm simply saying you want to look at the fundamental exchanges that take place in a negotiation and look for ways to claim your value. During a negotiation you are basically exchanging and revealing information, if you can discreetly add in the information on how valuable you are to them, then you can increase your chance at a better outcome for your negotiation.

There is a caveat here that I need to warn you about. While you want to reveal your value to the negotiator you also don't want to go to the other extreme and give away too much information. Don't give away your bottom line or allow the other party to know your walk away point. Think strategically about what information you want to release and when the best time is to release it. This can play an important part of negotiating and closing a good deal.

This goes along with the idea that in order to get a good deal everyone needs to benefit. Everyone needs to feel like they are getting a good deal from the negotiation. You don't want to come across as trying to be the best side, but you want the other party to feel they are going into the deal with a partner that is trying to find common ground for everyone involved.

Once you enter the negotiation, compare your preferences to the other party's. Before you can start to understand the goals of the other party, it is important that you have a clear goal of your own. To do this, I find it is best to identify the exact issues you're dealing with and then divide the issues into three categories: distributive, integrative or congruent. Distributive are problems where the other side has an opposing view. Integrative is problems where there are differences in views, but one side has assigned the problem greater value than the other party. Congruent is when there is no dispute to the problem by either side of the negotiation.

When you know exactly what type of issue you are dealing with it is a lot easier to develop a plan.

Once you have determined what you want and developed a detailed plan for going into the negotiation, a key decision to make is when you plan to make the first offer. I find myself faced with this question in every negotiation, and it all comes down to deciding whether you should make the first offer or wait to get an offer from the other party. I find that making the first offer provides you with a way to anchor the negotiations and have a great impact on the final deal. While there will still be a negotiation process, the facts show that the first offer has a great impact on the overall outcome of the negotiation. However, this doesn't mean you want to make the first offer in every negotiation.

You need to be aware that making the first offer also comes with the major disadvantage of revealing information to the other side that they can use against you later in the negotiation. Take the time to weigh the advantages and disadvantages of making the first offer during a negotiation. In general, I find that, if you are well prepared, you will be better off making the first offer and being prepared for what else may happen. However, if you aren't well prepared, then you may want to wait for the other side to make the first offer.

Lastly, when it comes to knowing what you want, I always advise people to know when it is best to simply walk away from the negotiation. If the terms offered are something below your bottom line then don't be afraid to refuse to sign. Don't be afraid to walk away from a deal that won't give you the deal you want. I like to think of negotiating like a game, and as long as you know the rules in advance, you can play the game well and have a better shot at winning.

If you win the game, then you want to get the verbal agreement in writing as soon as possible. If a negotiation takes place over several communications, make sure each one is documented with a recap of what was discussed. This way it will ensure that both parties are still in agreement once the deal is finished. Before signing at the end of the deal, make sure you also discuss how the agreement is concluded. In case the deal breaks down at this last critical moment, you want to make sure you have an exit strategy in place. All of this will help you to be best prepared for entering into a negotiation.

Chapter 5: Knowing What They Want

I've discussed what you need to know about yourself in order to be prepared. However, knowing what you want can only take you so far. In order to have a good chance to get what you want, you need to be prepared for everything the other side is going to throw your way. I find the best way to do this is by carefully planning and detailing exactly what the other side wants and how they are likely to go about getting it.

I've learned that the best way to start this process is to get into the mindset of the other negotiating party and know their thinking and position. You will be able to do this through research and analysis of the other party that you are going to be dealing with. Consider the following things I've learned that will help you be thoroughly prepared for any negotiation.

Most negotiators simply stop at the information I covered in the last chapter, they only consider what they want to get, what they are willing to give up, at what point they will walk away, and how they should go about the negotiation. However, I find that if you stop there, you are only going to be half prepared for a negotiation. If you take the time to go a step further by getting into the mindset of the other party, you are giving yourself a leg up on the competition.

You can't develop an effective strategy for negotiating if you don't develop an understanding of the other party you are dealing with. And without this strategy, you are dramatically reducing your chances of having a successful negotiation that ends in your favor. Let's take the time to break down the process of researching the other party and getting into their mindset so you can be properly prepared for a negotiation.

The first step in any detailed plan is that same as it was in the last chapter, know what the other party's interests are. Know their needs, aims, hopes, and concerns so you can not only know what they want to satisfy in a negotiation, but also know what is important to the other side. I find this is the most important step in any detailed plan that you need to carefully consider. If you don't propose an offer that reasonably satisfies the interests of the other party you are likely going to see the deal fail. The goal of any negotiation is to find a deal that will satisfy the interests of all parties involved. It is easy to see why it could be difficult to negotiate a deal if you don't know the interests of the other party.

4 STEPS TO KNOWING WHAT THEY WANT

Just consider the benefits you get by knowing the interests of the other party. You learn what you can offer that has value for the other party, which makes it easier for you to get what you want. It allows you to put together a deal that satisfies the other party's interests and means the deal is likely to be more sustainable. You will be able to increase your ability to find creative solutions and sources of value. You can avoid making a proposal that isn't likely to be accepted, so there is less time and frustration involved for both parties.

1. Identify Their Interests

To identify the interests of the other party, there are four steps I suggest you take. First, just take a few moments to brainstorm and write down any possible interests you can think of for the other party. Second, look at your list and prioritize them from most important to least. Third, compare their interests with your own and make a note of which interests are shared, conflicting, or just plain different. Fourth, prepare a list of questions and statements for each interest. Once you have done these four steps, you will have a complete and accurate list of the other party's interests that can help you get started in developing a detailed negotiation plan.

2. Indentify their Walk-Away Limit

The second step you need to take is to determine the likely walk-away limit of the other party. Just as you set your walk-away limit in the previous chapter, you know the other party is going to have the same limit. If the other party feels you aren't satisfying their interests, then they will do something else or possibly go with someone else who meets their interests. You don't want this walk-away alternative to mean they are walking away from a deal with you. Neither party is going to accept an offer that is worse than their walk-away limit, so if you know or at least have an idea of the other party's walk-away limit then you can stay within proper boundaries and have a better chance at closing the deal.

Consider the benefits you get from knowing this bit of information. You will have a more specific understanding of the choices the other party has for meeting their interests so you can have a clear path to making an offer that helps to close the deal. It will help give you a better sense of when they are bluffing so you can avoid giving up something valuable. Once you know their walk-away limit, you can carefully craft your arguments, so the alternative looks less appealing and increases the potential of your offer. You can determine ways to get the other party to avoid using their walk-away alternative.

To determine the other party's walk-away limit I have determined there are five steps you need to take. First, take a look at the list of interests again and make a list of alternatives that can meet those interests. Second, select the alternative that is most likely to satisfy the interest of the other party and you will know the likely walk-away limit for the other party. Third, determine just how well this alternative meets the interests of the other party. Fourth, put together a list of questions and/or statements that can help you determine whether or not you have found the right walk-away limit. Fifth, determine what you can do to limit the other party's ability to pursue this alternative and what you can say to make the alternative look less attractive to the other party.

One thing I've found through my experience is that all negotiators make the common mistake of assuming the other party can automatically agree to any deal. In fact, the opposite is often true. Often the parties involved in a negotiation are just there to explain and justify the recommended deal. It is difficult to have an effective negotiation if you don't know the level of authority of the other party and who they may have to negotiate with internally in order to close a deal. With some companies, they may even use this as a negotiation tactic.

There are numerous benefits you can get from just doing the simple research to determine the level of authority of the other negotiating party. You can avoid the tactics of dealing with a negotiating party that doesn't have proper authority and that will also reduce the time and frustration that comes along with it. If needed, you can know which parties to invite, so you have direct access to those in an authoritative position. You will know to escalate the negotiation process if you need to seek someone with more authority. If needed, you can prepare documents to help the other party in their internal negotiations. Lastly, it will make it easier to gauge the process you make during a negotiation so you can have an accurate timeline and expectation for the negotiation process.

3. Indentify the Decision Maker

When it comes to identifying authority, there are three steps I suggest you take. First, choose an agenda item within the first or second meeting that can help you clarify the authority of the other negotiating party. Second, based on the organization of the company you are dealing with you can assess who you need to have involved in order to get the deal evaluated and approved. Third, have a list of direct questions to ask about who has the authority to make the deal. If it isn't the person you are dealing with, then learn as much as you can about the deal process.

4. Indentify Their Strength and Weakness

The last part of getting to know what the other party wants is to consider their potential arguments, questions, and tactics. You will have a pretty clear picture of these things once you have done the previous steps of knowing the other party's interests, walk-away limit, and authority. The final step in the detailed plan is to understand their negotiation approach and what they are likely to say and do during the process. To do this, you want to focus on any arguments they are likely to make, what questions they might ask of you and what their likely tactics are going to be. You want to focus on these three things since they are the most likely to require a response from you.

Believe me... there is nothing worse than going into a negotiation and being surprised by a good argument, a single question or a tactic that destroys your plan. No matter what your reaction or response, it is going to be easier if you are properly prepared. When preparing for this part of the process, you want to pay extra attention to the arguments, questions and tactics you hope the other side won't use since these are likely to be the ones that will be used.

There are many benefits I found from preparing this part of your plan. Carefully preparing for counter-arguments based on your strengths and weaknesses is much better than relying on your ability to think quickly during a negotiation. You will have a clear plan of attack when it comes to knowing what information to share and what information to keep private. You can know the best way to respond to any tactics the other party might employ. You can prepare yourself to avoid giving any non-verbal cues that can undermine the negotiation process. It gives you a chance to role-play and decrease your chances of doing something that can undermine the negotiation process.

There are three steps I can offer to help with this step of the planning. First, brainstorm a list of any arguments, questions or tactics that the other party is likely to use that are difficult for you to respond to. Second, based on everything you learned about the other party at the first stages of this planning process you want to add to this list more arguments, questions and tactics that you would be likely to use if you were in their position. Third, prepare and practice. Lots of preparation and practice. This is the only way to be truly prepared for anything that may come your way.

Now that you have the four steps to discovering what the other party wants, you can develop a well thought out plan that helps you prepare for any negotiation process. However, I have a few additional tips to offer you that can really help you get a leg up on the competition. Take the time to talk with others who have negotiated or worked with the other party in the negotiation since they have likely learned some valuable tips to help you. Another source of information is to talk to individuals who have the same role in your organization as that of the other party you will be negotiating with. Use your marketing department or hire a researcher to find any industry research, reports or intelligence on the other party. Take the time to do your own research on the other party. You would be surprised what information you can get simply by visiting a website or doing a little reading in publications related to the industry.

Remember it is entirely up to you to determine how much time and effort you want to put into preparing a detailed plan for your negotiation. However, I'm speaking from experience when I tell you that following the steps in this chapter and the previous chapters will go a long way to giving you a leg up and a better shot at closing deal that gets you what you want.

Chapter 6: Knowing When to Walk Away

When it comes to negotiations, I'm big on stressing the importance of preparations. Most people have the impression that negotiators talk fast, play tricks and do anything in order to close a deal. The real negotiation process and those who do it is far from this mainstream picture. While planning to close a deal is important, the fact is that it's just as important to be prepared to walk away from the deal.

Walking away from a deal during negotiation is something few negotiators want to do, since it is similar to setting the reset button on the entire process. After so much work has been put into planning and working on getting the best deal, the last thing most negotiators want to do is walk away. However, you can increase your confidence by always remembering that there is another option available to you. I find by keeping an open mind you are able to improve the quality of your deals.

However, it isn't that easy to simply pick a time to walk away from a deal. In the business industry, you have to be careful not to ruin relationships that you may need in the future, but you also don't want to end up closing the deal on a contract that isn't ideal. That is why I want to spend some time talking about how you can be prepared for walking away from a negotiation.

Again, I stress the importance of planning. Knowledge gives you the information needed to fare better in negotiations. Before you start any negotiation, you want to research and carefully consider all the possible outcomes. Just as I've stressed with all the other chapters. When it comes to determining your walk away point, the focus of your research should be on the price you can afford and value of all the different options available to you. There are often a number of features available during a deal as well, so you want to know what interests you and what you are likely not to need that can be taken out of a deal.

When it comes to negotiating, you will often find yourself at a disadvantage if you simply focus on one number. With all your focus and attention on one goal, you can easily end up making a worse deal than you think you should. When you focus on all the options available, you stand a better chance of steering the negotiation towards an outcome that benefits you and your business. However, you also need to be careful and be prepared to make the crucial step of walking away if the negotiation starts to shift way from a good deal for you and your business. I know you are all thinking the same thing I was when I first started... how do I know it's time to walk away? To determine this, I need to discuss something called a zone of agreement.

All parties entering a negotiation have already established their desired outcome and a worst-case scenario. When you go into a negotiation, you want to not only know your desired outcomes, but also the lowest deal you are willing to accept. If you are acting as the buyer, you want to have a desired low purchase price, but you also want to know the highest price you are willing to pay in a worst case scenario.

A zone of agreement is the area between the worst-case scenarios for both parties. This is why you risk walking away with a bad deal if you haven't determined your worst-case scenario before going into a negotiation. If you aren't prepared, it is always best to walk away from a deal. When it comes to walking away, you need to have an established BATNA or Best Alternative to a Negotiated Agreement. This way you can make a final offer before walking away.

Never reveal your BATNA early in the negotiations. If you do this, you will reduce the weight of having a last minute offer and the option of an alternative. You don't want to lose your last minute negotiating tool, and this would mean you lose all bargaining tools. There are three simple steps that I recommend you use to establish your BATNA before starting a negotiation.

3 STEPS TO ESTABLISHING YOUR BATNA

1. Know your Price Range

First, you need to know your acceptable price range. While a seller is going to want the highest possible price and a buyer is going to want the lowest possible price, if you focus on just this one point then you won't be able to tell how far you are moving away from it during negotiations. Rather calculate a value that you are willing to accept. When you have a range going into a negotiation, you have a little bit of room to maneuver.

2. Know Their Price Range

Second, determine the acceptable range of the other party. In order to know how strong your BATNA is going to be, you also need to have an understanding of the other party's acceptable range. There are a number of resources that can help you determine the value of nearly anything.

3. Know the Deal Breaker List

Third, you need to establish a list of deal breakers. Price isn't the only thing you are focused on during a negotiation. Take the time to consider a list of unacceptable conditions before you start negotiating. If you are presented with one of the deal breakers on your list then simply walk away from the deal.

Even if you find yourself in a walk-away situation, always remember to do it in a civil and courteous manner. In the business world, you don't want to sever all ties completely, since you may find yourself working with that individual or company again at some point. Sometimes I even find a person may call me back with a better deal simply because I walked away and left things on good terms.

So if you realize the negotiation has moved beyond your acceptable range, and you don't get the other party to accept your BATNA; then simply thank them for their time, shake hands and walk away from the deal. This will give the other party a powerful statement that shows you are confident and have integrity. Even if you don't close the deal with the person, you will have successfully left them with a picture of yourself as an honorable person.

This doesn't mean you are going to walk away from every negotiation, but you do need to be prepared to do so, and know you have that option. Before you even start a negotiation you want to have a walk away point established since it gives you the confidence needed to have a strong negotiation. When you are prepared for the negotiation and the possibility of walking away, then you will be able to do so without getting scared, flustered or frustrated with the negotiation process.

Know the worst case scenario for both yourself and the other party and have an established list of deal breakers. This way you have a clearly established zone of agreement. If you don't get an offer within your acceptable range, then offer your BATNA and if this doesn't work, simply walk away amicably. You will be surprised how you feel after walking away from a negotiation.

Chapter 7: Know How Much to Compromise

Compromise is something you have to get used to during any negotiation. I find you almost always have to give up something you want in order to get something of more importance or value. You will typically find compromise occurring in win-lose situations. While neither side is going to get the fixed size of the pie they want, both will have to make appropriate concessions in order to reach an acceptable agreement.

When it comes to negotiating with a compromise, there are two principle ways you can do it. The first way is for both parties to go back and forth with various offers and concessions until an agreement is reached at some point in the middle. This often occurs with a specific issue, like a price. However, if multiple issues are being negotiated, then additional compromises are necessary. The basic idea is for each side to give up something to other side that they don't really care about.

However, I have found that there are times when some things can't be compromised because they ask a person or business to give up too much. I find the two most common things that can't be compromised are values and fundamental human needs. Usually, individuals and businesses won't make a deal if they have to compromise either of these.

There are some that believe you can try an integrative or interest-based negotiation in which you can find a win-win solution for both sides without having to make a compromise as long as individuals are open about their real wants and needs. In this situation, I feel you don't need to make concessions as much as you often do when doing a negotiation.

This is often because compromise is perceived differently depending on the culture. For example, in the United States compromise is often seen as a bad thing, while some traditional cultures such as Hawaiian culture view compromise as an important way to end a conflict. Therefore, the culture will play a big role in how much compromise needs to be made.

Chapter 8: Knowing the Barrier

When it comes to trying to have a successful negotiation, the biggest issue is barriers. I find there are quite a few barriers that can come up and block effective communication. In order for a negotiation to be successful, you need to have everyone able to hear and understand what is being said. An agreement can only stem from understanding. However, this can all be destroyed by barriers, whether they are real, created or perceived. Barriers can be verbal or non-verbal. Some are easier to overcome than others. Although I believe that once you have a handle on barriers, you will stand a better chance at a successful negotiation.

The first thing you need to do is learn to identify barriers. When you can identify different barriers you can know how to remove them so your message is both heard and understood. To identify barriers you not only need to be a skilled communicator, but you also observant. Observe how the other party reacts to what you are saying and make sure they are listening. This way you can be sure they understand your message. However, if you notice they are wandering or disconnecting, then chances are that they do not understand what you are saying, and you need to regain their focus.

The simplest and often most effective way I've found to regain their focus is to simply stop speaking. Once the other party has realized that you are no longer speaking, you can then resume your conversation as if nothing has happened. Although, depending on the situation, you may also need to call their attention to the fact that they weren't listening to you and ask them what the problem may be. While this may come across as rude, it can often be the best way to determine what the barrier is so that you can remove it and move forward with the negotiation. Always remember that if communications aren't being heard, then it is best to wait until the other party is ready or capable of hearing and understanding.

As I said earlier, barriers of all types exist. They can be tangible or intangible, imagined or real. Barriers can also be caused by a variety of things. 7 most common barriers include the following:

1. Language differences

2. Culture differences

3. Physical barriers

4. Personal problems

5. Preconceived notions

6. Reputation

7. Exhaustion

If you can get the other party to acknowledge barriers to the communication process, then you can use this as an opportunity to agree on a way to resolve the barriers. This will make it easier to resolve real issues and get on with the negotiation process.

Anything can block communications, from poor equipment to people who aren't good at speaking. However, the most difficult barriers are internal psychological barriers that prevent people from hearing what the other party is saying. People often hear what they want to hear in order to meet their expectations. These barriers are often developed from past experiences, education and basic needs. These don't come from facts, but rather from personal perceptions.

If you find yourself speaking to a large group of people you need to keep these personal perceptions in mind since each person is likely to hear something different based on their own unique personal perceptions. It is really difficult to change these personal perceptions, so you simply need to overcome these barriers by validating what is being heard and make sure everyone is getting the same understanding.

I find there are three ways you can do this. One, you can ask follow-up questions. Two, you can observe the other party's reaction to what is being said. Third, you can restate the most important parts and ask for confirmation.

However, don't just focus on the other party. Keep in mind that you are also filtering the information you are receiving. This part of listening occurs in your subconscious. In order to become a skilled negotiator, you need to filter what you hear from what is really being said, by using the same information only in reverse.

There is a lot of work that goes into breaking down communications barriers. You are basically trying to get past decades of learned behavior that people are often unaware of.

Then there are barriers that are created. There may be a time when either side wants to slow down the negotiation process through the use of time-buying techniques. The most common way to do this is through the creation of a communication barrier. However, I find that as we get more and more into a society that expects everyone to be the best at what they do, this type of negotiating tactic isn't used as commonly anymore.

However, I find it still remains an effective tactic. If you need to ask a question or get clarification, there is nothing wrong with that. If you are in an argument with another individual, you can ask for clarification which will break their train of thought and give you time to think of a way to defuse the situation.

On the other hand, you may be doing your negotiations by email or fax. If this is the case, you can simply wait a few days to respond. When you do this, you are sending the message that you are too busy, you don't find it important, it never arrived or that you just aren't ready to respond. However, don't let these perceptions rush you into making a decision. Time can often be used to your advantage in negotiations. Often if you take the time to consider a deal the other party may get nervous and offer something better. This is also an excellent way of determining how badly the other party wants to make an agreement.

When it comes to negotiating, I find it's not IF but WHERE the barriers exist. Once you find a barrier, you need to uncover it and understand where the other party is coming from. This goes back to my earlier chapters and why it is important to get to know a person before entering negotiations. This background information will help keep your alert to communication barriers. When you find a barrier, you need to overcome it.

If the barrier is something physical like a language or cultural barrier, then you may need to get a co-negotiator to change the image. If the barrier is more technical in nature, like equipment issues, then you need to call in an expert.

However, ingrained perception is more difficult to remove. To overcome these barriers, the first step is to demonstrate that you have their trust. You can't do this quickly or easily since you need to demonstrate through your performance that you are someone who can be trusted again. When you know the barriers then you can do something to overcome them. Some are simple to change, while others will require a lot of work to overcome.

When it comes to dealing with a business, the most common barrier is not dealing with the person who has the authority to do anything. However, this is often a simple barrier to overcome since you simply need to make sure you are negotiation with someone in a position of authority.

As you progress in your business negotiations, it will get easier to identify and overcome challenges. So simply practice and prepare ahead of time and eventually you will find yourself identifying and overcoming communication barriers without even knowing you are doing it.

Chapter 9: Knowing How to Control Your Emotion

As you have likely grasped from the previous chapters, a lot of emotions go into negotiations. These emotions can have both positive and negative effects on a negotiation. Emotions can either lead to heated negotiations, or they can cause people to freeze up and the negotiations stall. It entirely depends on the type of person involved in the negotiation.

There are individuals who are positively terrified of having to negotiate and will do anything to avoid the experience, even if it means quickly taking a deal. These individuals aren't competitive and sometimes aren't cooperative when it comes to negotiating. Rather they just want to avoid it, and as long as their minimum goal is met, then they will sign a deal just to get it over with. This is especially true if the other party has an agenda or style different from them. As you can imagine, this is a very expensive individual to have at the negotiating table.

I find the one thing that makes the difference between closing a deal and becoming deadlocked is poise. This is the ability to keep your head, no matter what personality styles you work with. It all comes down to the ability to keep your emotions in check during the negotiation process.

Most research on negotiation tends to present emotion as a barrier to reaching a deal. Most negotiators advise new people to separate the person from the problem and take a very analytic approach to negotiating, rather than a personal approach. Preparation and planning is a crucial part of any negotiation. It is important to know the core interests, the walk away options, and the choices available. Having the numbers and knowing the marketplace in advance is certainly important before entering a negotiation. It all makes sense to have plans in place to get through a negotiation. However, I feel this is only half of the negotiation process.

I find that passions and emotions play a role in negotiation whether you want them to or not. Emotions are certainly an important part of dispute resolution, and this can happen in a number of negotiations. The key is learning to channel and benefit from your emotions in order to successfully engage others and adapt to the situation at hand. This means before you start to negotiate you need to prepare yourself emotionally. Even if a negotiation seems to be going smoothly, a number of emotions may be lurking just below the surface. If you don't address these emotions, it can build and affect your relationship with the other party which can, in turn, jeopardize your ability to close a deal.

Chapter 10: Using the Time (Clock) to Your Advantage

When it comes to negotiating, I have found a powerful tool to apply to your strategic advantage is deadlines. If your negotiation stalls, the best way to move it forward is to use deadlines. You may find yourself bargaining for months with no end in sight. But with a critical deadline approaching, you will be able to reach a deal within the final moments. If there is no deadline to worry about, negotiators may try to use stalling tactics in order to pressure the other party into giving in and taking the deal.

However, I find that while deadlines are an effective tool for negotiations, they are also a very misunderstood strategy. A lot of negotiators I've worked with don't like to place a deadline on their deals. For one thing, when you have a deadline you are reducing your freedom and putting pressure on yourself as well as the other side to reach an agreement. So while a deadline can be beneficial for you, the fact is that using a shared deadline to pressure the other party can have a negative impact on you as well. Therefore, the first step you need to take is to decide whether or not to use deadlines when negotiating.

When deciding whether or not to use deadlines, you need to avoid making the biggest mistake that many negotiators make; you don't want to focus on how a deadline will affect you without determining how it will affect the other side. The most effective negotiators realize that deadlines affect everyone equally, but can be valuable to when defusing stalling tactics.

Often you can defuse stalling tactics by simply stating that you have a deadline at the start of the negotiation process. Since deadlines put pressure on everyone at the table, they can get negotiations moving again. Therefore, don't be afraid to use deadlines and commit to them as long as you can use them to your advantage.

Once you've decided whether or not to use deadlines, you need to take the next step in determining whether or not to disclose your deadlines. Many negotiators view deadlines as a weakness and therefore fail to disclose it to the other side. However, I find this strategy will put you in the worst possible position. I find that when you hide a deadline you are greatly increasing your risk of stalling the process.

Hiding a deadline will also make you accelerate your negotiations, causing you to make concessions. On the other side of the table, your counterpart will think you don't have a deadline so they will try to hold out and wait for you to concede. This means you are highly unlikely to reach an agreement before time runs out and even if you do reach a deal you are likely to get a negative outcome.

Take the time to notify your opponent of any deadlines and you are likely to get a better deal. Why is this? For one thing is means both sides are more likely to work towards an agreement in order to avoid the deadline, which means you are less like to use your walk away strategy and get nothing. Making deadlines known also means that the other side is going to make concessions more quickly. Therefore, I think it's a good idea to notify the other side of deadlines.

However, I need to caution you on two things before you determine whether or not to disclose your deadlines. First, you don't want to confuse deadlines with time costs. A deadline is going to end the negotiation for both parties, while a time cost will apply to only one party or the other. Try to impose a deadline only if it affects both parties.

The second cautionary note is to consider whether or not you want to tell your BATNA at the same time you make a deadline. If you have a strong BATNA, you may want to tell it to the other party. However, if your BATNA is weak, then you may want to keep it a secret. It is possible to conceal your BATNA while still telling them of your final deadline. A deadline doesn't necessarily mean you have a weak bargaining position. In fact, I find the opposite is often true, and those with the tightest deadlines have the best BATNA's.

You will have plenty of opportunities to use deadlines to your strategic advantage so don't be afraid to set a deadline and reveal it to the other party.

Chapter 11: Finding Mutual Gain

When it comes to negotiations, you can take a collaborative approach to mutual gains negotiations. Rather than the standard adversarial approach or the win-lose approach, the mutual gains approach focuses on a process of consensus building to get a win-win approach. Mutual gains negotiations are only successful if both parties have a shared understanding of the project scope and complexity. By agreeing to a goal of a mutually beneficial solution, then both parties will be able to trust each other.

5 BASIC PRINCIPLES OF MUTUAL GAIN NEGOTIATIONS

1. Indentifying Mutual Interest

The first step is for both parties to identify their interests. It is also important for both sides to try and understand the interests of the other side. An interest can be a number of things including needs, concerns, motives, goals, objectives or any combination of these.

2. Willingness to Work Together

Second, both sides need to work together to consider all options available to them. This will take creativity and an open mind in order to find all the options that can lead to a mutually acceptable solution that will meet the interests of both sides.

3. Agreeing on Standards

Third, both sides need to agree on standards or criteria. With these established, consensus building becomes easier. Discussions can be more focused on facts rather than opinions.

4. All Options on the Table

Fourth, make sure all alternatives are on the table. Both sides need to have an established BATNA, and they need to be open about this so that everyone knows the fallback position in case the negotiations fail.

5. Build a Relationship

Fifth, build a relationship. Negotiations should have no personal problems and focus entirely on the business aspect. The goal of mutual gains negotiations is to build and strengthen the relationship between both sides. Both sides need to have honest and open communications. When communications are based on facts and not opinions, then the relationship will grow, and the negotiation will have a better outcome.

In order for mutual gains negotiations to be successful, both parties need to work together to make sure they agree on the scope of services, project complexity and deliverables before any proposals can be generated.

There are four steps needed to be successful with these negotiations.

4 STEPS TO A WIN-WIN FOR BOTH PARTIES

1. Good Preparation

As with all the other chapters, I've always stressed preparation as the first and most important step. Both sides can prepare by understanding the interests and alternatives of the other side. Having a good BATNA on the table can help both sides work together toward a common agreement.

2. Create Value

The second step is for each side to create value. This can be done by inventing something without committing. Basically, both sides need to advance options that appeal to the interests of the other party. Often by discussing various value options, both parties can discover more interests and create options that may not have been previously considered in order to reach a common agreement.

3. Coming to an Agreement

At some point in the process, both sides need to come to a final agreement. The more value you can create in the third step, the easier the fourth step will be. The key during this finalizing process is to avoid going into positional bargaining. It is best for both parties to divide the value by finding objective criteria that all parties can use. When these criteria or principles support the allocation decisions, then both parties can have a stability of agreements and increase the chances of an effective deal.

4. Forecast Future Challenges

Lastly, both parties need to brainstorm any possible future challenges and a solution to them. Often when difficult negotiations near the end, something can go wrong. That is why it is important to take this final step by strengthening the agreement with a list of possible things that can go wrong and ways to solve them. While this may seem like a difficult and unnecessary step, it can make the difference between finalizing a deal and having to walk away.

Chapter 12: Make Them Look Good, Let Them Brag

Negotiations can be difficult. You may not feel like you are getting what you want. Or perhaps you're like me, tired of dealing with the demanding or manipulative personalities. One way I've found to overcome this is by developing a relationship during the negotiation process. When you build trust with the other party, then you will be benefiting both sides. The key to building this trust is to pay attention to and focus on the other party. There are a few ways you can do this.

6 WAYS TO MAKE THEM LOOK GOOD

1. Win-Win Situation

First, try not to approach the negotiation as a win-lose situation. If you do this, then the other party may feel like they are losing and as a result, may choose not to fulfill their part of the bargain. In fact, both sides often can't win since the interests of both parties are rarely the same. So you may want to consider partnering with the other side to have a win-win approach to the negotiation.

2. Allow Participation

Second, you want to make sure you allow the other side to participate. Everyone wants to be involved in a decision that is going to affect them and this is why it is important to find what the other party wants. Take the time to find this out by asking for their opinions and advice while also understanding their fears and concerns. View the deal from the perspective of the other party in order to see what they will view as benefits and drawbacks.

3. Acknowledge Their Interest

Third, you want to acknowledge the interests of the other party. When you demonstrate that you know the other side's situation you are developing a relationship and building trust. You will also want to state your own interests so that everyone is on equal ground.

4. Offer Options

Fourth, you want to have plenty of options available. Take the time to think of as many options as possible so you can go into the negotiations with plenty of ideas. This way you can present yourself as working to find a deal that works for both parties.

5. Offer to Help

Fifth, offer to help the other party. Even after you reach an agreement, decisions still need to be made. Offer to help the other party research these decisions to make the process easier for them.

6. Make them Look Good

Lastly, you want to make the other side look good. Often times if you aren't dealing with someone in authority then they are going to need to sell the negotiation to their boss. To help with this, you want to give the right facts and documentation needed to convince the people in authority to make the deal, so try to give them all the tools and tricks they need to convince their superiors.

Remember that whether or not you liked your counterpart at the beginning of the deal, you will likely have a bigger dislike for them at the end of the negotiation. Yet it is important to make the other party look good and let them brag in order to ratify the deal.

Chapter 13: The Power of Paper

Congratulations are in order. You have successfully made it to the end of the negotiations and are in the home stretch. So now what do you need to do. In this chapter we will discuss the final part of the process, signing the agreement.

Even after you've reached an agreement you want to make sure you finalize as soon as possible. There are 3 tactics I've found that can be very helpful.

3 WAYS YOU CAN PUT PAPER POWER TO WORK FOR YOU

1. Following up

First, it can be a good idea to send a follow-up email with a summary to the other party. While verbal contracts are binding, you still want to get written proof as soon as possible. A verbal contract will still be held to terms, but you still want to follow up through an email as soon as negotiations are finished. You can thank your counterpart for the negotiation and summarize what you discussed. A reply will give you the written proof you need before signing a contract, and it can help avoid last minute conflicts.

2. Show a Summery Deal

Second, in order to make your counterpart feel like they made the right choice you should compliment them on their negotiating skills. While the numbers and facts are an important part of the negotiation, an even stronger factor is the human emotional factor. Hand them a copy of a summary of the deal, highlighting what they have gained from this deal. If you want to make them feel even better, give them a copy of your initial offerings too... this way they see how far you have come up to meet their offer. Make yourself look like a loser. Trust me it will make them feel really good.

Everyone has a perceived notion of how they did in a negotiation, but when you compliment the other party you are making them more likely to sign the paperwork and want to negotiate with you again the future.

3. Sign the Purchase Agreement

Third, you want to make sure you are the first person in a negotiation to write up a contract. Not only does this allow you to solidify the deal more quickly, but it also gives you the option to create any default options. Often when the other party comes across an option that is chosen by default, they will simply accept it. This means that when you draft the contract, you will be able to control the terms. However, this doesn't mean you should be manipulative and sneak other terms into the agreement, but you can mention additional items and since they will be a default the other side is more likely to accept them.

Now you are done with the negotiation process and have a signed deal. Congratulations! Now get out there and do it again!

Chapter 14: A Deal I Recently Negotiated

As I mentioned early in the book, 2 years ago I got involved in consulting business when a group of investors asked my help to negotiate a 2 gas station package deal on their behalf. It took 3 long months to complete but at the end I was able to get a very good deal negotiated for them.

Let me give you some background on the sellers and a brief summary of the deal.

The seller is a family owned fuel distributors/oil company. They were trying to sell 5 of their stores in one particular city, where 3 of those 5 were already sold, and my clients were trying to buy the remaining two.

As soon as I agreed to help my investors, I went to work, and my first step was to gather as much data as I could about the business and the sellers.

HERE IS A LIST OF MY FINDINGS:

About the Businesses

- Both properties are great properties but looked little dated and neglected

- Both stores had a laundry list of maintenance issues (revealed after a professional inspection)

- Employees showed very low morale due to lack of support from the management

- Declining sales

- Poor merchandising

- Absence of competitive product and fuel pricing

I also researched both the actual value of the property and some comparable sales of nearby gas stations.

About the Seller

- A family owned oil company owned by two brothers

- The owners are located about 300 miles from the city where these 2 gas stations are located.

- One of the brothers went to the same college as I did

- Both brothers are close to my age

- They own 17 very high volume gas stations in and around their hometown

- They are financially very strong and not suffering from any cash flow issue

After the initial contact via email, I received the last 2 years of sales data along with some financial reports on the store. I briefly reviewed them and identified some questionable numbers and made notes about them. I then asked for a meeting.

The first meeting was a brief one, where we met at one of the locations, and they handed me more documents about the stores and showed me around. I expressed my concerns about some of their financial records and they explained them.

Since this deal through a business broker we knew their asking price, but during the first visit I did ask about the price and got the same number as the broker gave us. I did this to verify that there was no error in pricing between what the broker said vs. what the sellers said.

After we had toured the stores, we went and sat in a Dunkin' Donuts where I brought up our college and we talked a lot about our new football team, overall college life, what we did and all that. I did not bring up the business at all. We also spoke about our kids, life in general and work, and as they were about to leave, they invited me back to their city for lunch one day. I told them I would love to join them in two weeks. Since both of the brothers were very open and talkative, I decided to listen more and understand them and their personality rather than doing most of the talking myself. So throughout this meeting I was not the one striking up the conversation

Over the next two weeks, I stayed busy laying out a detailed plan on how and what I would be negotiating with them.

11 STEP PREPARATION BEFORE THE MEETING

1. Using all the comparable sales data for other stores in the area, I narrowed all of the options down to two properties that shared many similarities with the two properties I would be negotiating.

2. I visited both of the properties and noted down all the issues I found from my visit, along with what the professional inspection had found.

3. After analyzing their financials, I prepared two projected P&L for each store. The first one showed that the store was barely breaking even with the sales trend that each had. The second showed that if we made some significant changes, it could show some profit in the long run, although nothing will happen in the short term(within first 3-6 months)

4. I prepared a list of repairs, upgrades, and changes for each store that were required and or needed immediately

5, I then asked two different contractors to quote those repairs, upgrades, and changes and so had two different estimates in my hand.

6. Without revealing the seller's actual asking price, let's say hypothetically the sellers were asking 2.2 million for both properties. After talking to my investors, discussing all the work that needed to be done on those properties, all the comp sales and with the weak financial numbers, we decided to start at 1.6 million and not to go over 1.8 million as our final offering price for both stores.

7. I also looked at the other 3 stores they sold recently and found out in all 3 stores, the difference between asking price and finals selling price was about $130,000-$165,000, meaning they agreed to reduce the price by that much at the end, so I knew they are willing to negotiate, and it was not a fixed price.

8. I also prepared a list of documents I needed from them, including the tank registration, UST (underground storage Tank) yearly testing reports, and some sales breakdowns I noticed that were missing in their financial reports. I didn't really need any of these items, but this was a way to buy some time to counter an offer in the event they did not agree with my offer.

9. I prepared a set of purchase agreements but left the price blank. I also attached a power of attorney along with it from my investors to me, so the sellers knew I had the authority to negotiate on the investors' behalf.

10. I drew up an offer letter with two options. One, a price for both As Is and the 2nd option was a price where they fixed all the issues.

11. The last thing I did was a SWOT analysis of the seller and the properties, something I practice for any new businesses that I am looking to buy, lease or help any investors to acquire. This should the last part of your research and done only after you collected all the data I mentioned at the beginning of the book.

SWOT Analysis Findings

S= Strength Of the seller

The sellers are financially strong and not suffering from cash flow issue

The sellers have experience in this line of business

W=Weakness of the seller

The stores are too far away for them to manage properly

The employee morale seems to be very low

Stores are not profitable due to lack of merchandising and marketing efforts

Numerous maintenance issues at both locations

O=Opportunity for us

That the sellers are not local and have limited control over the stores due to the distance

Both businesses are showing signs of downward sales volume

The employees are showing low morale

Stores are suffering from too many maintenance issues

T=Threat for the sellers

Fear of losing more sales volume

Fear of employees leaving to find steadier jobs

A few of the maintenance issues becoming severe and ending up costing a lot of money

Downward sales volume would also reduce the business value over time

Once I knew their SWOT analysis result, I knew how much I could influence and or manipulate their decision-making process, as long as I had a decent offer and could make them understand we were serious, capable and genuinely interested in buying their business for the right price.

I also knew since these two are the remaining ones, I had a better chance of getting them to come down even lower than what they did for the other previous buyers.

Now some of you may wonder why on earth, if the stores were losing or at a break-even, would a group of investors want to buy such properties. It was because these properties were at prime locations, and had great potential to do great. Not to mention that they could generate revenue/rent for many years to come, so they are actually great income producing properties for most long-term investors.

If you read or listen to any of my podcasts, I have argued for many years that gas station business is one of the very few truly recession-proof businesses out there. Not to mention the demand for these businesses are very high, and the failure rate is relatively very low.

Let's get back to the point. The day of the meeting, I traveled to their city and met them at their office. Both brothers were present and greeted me warmly. They gave me a tour of their office and introduced me to their staff, and then again they started off talking about their college days, and I mentioned to them that I ran into a marketing professor recently at a seminar who remembeeds both of the brothers and sent his regards. They were surprised to know that the professor even remembeeds them both. It sure made them happy.

After enjoying some coffee, they invited me to their conference room where the actual negotiation/business talk would take place. They asked me if I had any more questions or needed any more documents, to which I handed them the list I prepared and told them they could send these to me whenever they could get them ready, but didn't have to rush into it today.

I then asked them what they thought about their stores and how much do they thought they should be sold for, though I knew the answer. I wanted them to get into the frame of mind and fathom the high dollar figures they were asking, and to my surprise the older brother started telling me he knew of some issues that their stores were facing and, being so far away they just thought the stores were being managed properly and if I was serious, they want to make a deal sooner rather than later.

I assured them that the investors I represent were serious buyers, and that was why I was there, traveling all the way to their city.

The next thing the older brother said was truly an approach to close to deal in good faith. He offered to sell both for $2.1

million, and so before I even started with my negotiation, he reduced the price by $100,000.

I told him we were "we are getting close but not enough" then I took out the list of repair, upgrade, and changes that needed to be done, regardless if we buy it or if they kept the stores. I showed them the list along with two of the estimates which were right around $87,000(the difference between the two estimates were about $6500).

We then discussed few of those items, and I realized they were not even aware of some of the issues I listed.

Next, I brought out the P&L I prepared based on their actual sales and expenses. In mine it showed loss and in theirs showed some profit, and before they could disagree I pointed out to them that in their P&L there was no mortgage/note payment to the bank since these, I assumed, were paid off properties. But in our case, there would be a note payment. I then jokingly told them it is hard to find buyers who have 2 million cash to buy gas stations, so whoever they find will likely to have a bank note/mortgage.

At this point they asked me if I had any offer in mind. My response was sure that was why I was there. With that, I took out my offer letter with two options, and I handed a copy to each brother. The first option of the offer was for $1.5

million where we do all the repairs, or the 2nd option was $1.6 million where they would have to do all the repairs.

At this point, I casually mentioned to them that I looked at few comparable sales in the area for the last year, and showed them some examples of them. I emphasized to them that, in order for a bank to loan the funds, it has to make sense for the bank, and it had to have enough income generation so these properties can sustain a loan payment and still make money.

Then I had to excuse myself to make an important personal phone call and went out of their office and sat in my car. I just wanted to give them some time to digest the low offer.

When I went back, I knew they were little disappointed and little heartbroken. Instead of talking about my offer I started asking them how they were able to manage stores so far away and praised them for doing a good job for so many years. I told them they have the power and knowledge that I lack when it comes to managing retail businesses remotely.

After a few minutes of such discussion, I told them that I needed to get back and if they needed to think about it for a few days that can do so, then casually mentioned that I was looking at another package deal for my investors and had to travel some distance again that same week to another city (which was not really true).

As I was leaving, they both came out to my car and I told them if we could make the deal it will be a win-win for both of us, as they can finally close the chapter of running long distance businesses and can sleep better at night. I also informed them that for an average Joe, it would be hard to get a loan to buy their businesses, as they were both at the break-even point, and banks don't loan money to break-even businesses. But I assured them that my investors had a line of credit from a major bank, so if we agree on the price we could close the deal in less than 30 days, when, for an average Joe it can take up to 3-4 months to get a loan approved from most banks.

The next day I got a call from the older brother, and he explained that he had an extensive discussion with his brother, and they both agreed that the offer was too low, but if we could work towards a middle and more agreeable point, then they can still do the deal.

I then told him that I too had talks with my investors and told them about our meetings and told them how I enjoyed visiting at their office and how hospitable they were. I then told them I tried to convince the investors to raise the offer so the seller can justify selling to us, and then told the older brother that my investors agreed to raise both the offers by $50,000(Option A &B) and that was the best they could do considering the risk and the work that are involved in both stores.

I knew if I could show good faith they would come up with a more reasonable number and they did. He right way offered me $1.85 million for option A (Where we do all the upgrades and repairs) which was $250,000 less than what he first offered at his office. So at this point, the difference between our offer which was $1.55 million and their counter which was $1.85 million was $300,000.

I told him that I would have to get back to him as I would have to talk to my investors. I waited two days and no, I didn't talk to my investors. I just wanted to give them some time so they would know I was not in any hurry. When I called them, the older brother answered, and he sounded anxious, I apologized for the delay in calling him back and told him I was busy working on another deal.

I then broke the news that my investors could only afford to sweeten the deal by going up another $75,000 for option A, and that was our final offer. I also told him since my investors were looking at another package deal they would have to know the answer by the next day. If not they would move on to the next deal as the risks were too high in this deal.

Then I again apologized for not being able to raise the price for them and told them they have a great business sense and even if we don't get to do the deal, they will find another buyer or they can just hire some good managers and run the stores themselves and make more money. I even offered to help them in merchandising and marketing aspect of the stores in the event they did decide to keep the stores.

The older brother sounded somewhat disappointed and asked me again if we could meet them "halfway". My response was "I tried, but they don't want to go up any higher than they already have." He understood and told me he would call me back the next day.

He was man of his word. He called me in the morning and told me his other brother does not want to do the deal as our offer was too low and they had two other offers both of which were higher than ours, but both of those buyers wanted 3 months to close the deal as they would have to apply and get a loan approved from the bank.

Once again I told him I was not able to convince my investors, as I again spoke to them the night before but their answer was the same. I told him I was sorry and wished them good luck and told them we would do another deal with them in the future, as I was trying to end the conversation. He finally gave in and told me the only way he would agree to my price is if I was willing to pay all the closing costs, and he wouldn't have to pay a penny.

I told him I didn't discuss the closing costs with my investors but I will take it upon myself and if they didn't pay, I would pay out of my commission as I felt bad for negotiating so hard with them.

He was finally relieved, and so was I. We ended up closing the deal in less than 25 days for exactly $1.625 Million, and we did pay the closing cost, but it wasn't much at all.

I did take some risk making this deal happen, but I only took calculated risk. I knew their situation and the only reason I knew was because of the research I had done before meeting them.

Did I follow all my 13 tips and tricks? I sure did, but not all of them at once. I took bits and pieces from each and used it as I needed, but not in any particular order.

Just remember there is no cookie cutter method that you can learn and apply in every business negotiation, they will vary widely based on many factors. But as long as you can master these 13 skills and know them by heart, when the time comes you will know which to use and when to use them.

It is an art, and if you can master the skills, you will be an artist.

www.ingramcontent.com/pod-product-compliance
Lightning Source LLC
Chambersburg PA
CBHW060403190526
45169CB00002B/737